Precious Prayers For My Wedding

Photo

A threefold cord is not quickly broken.

Ecclesiastes 4:12

*A*s far back as you can remember, you prayed for him—the man of your dreams who would guide you through life as a leader, lover, and friend. Now the dream is real, and in mere moments the hopes and plans of a lifetime will be met in the arms of the man waiting for you at the end of the aisle. As a million thoughts flood your mind in these emotional and life-changing moments, know that peace comes in remembering.

Long before you knew this man, God chose him—just for you. Faithfully, God fashioned in him the character He knew you'd need to discover the deeper aspects of God's heart. In His time, He brought you two together. God is the unseen link that binds your hearts together both today—and for the rest of your lives. As God has always been your strength and hope, He will be still. *Precious Prayers For My Wedding* is uniquely designed to help you draw on that strength during this sacred time in your life. While the pastel illustrations by renowned artist Sam Butcher capture the beauty and innocence of this union, select Scripture verses complete the picture of God's presence and importance in the ceremony and life to come. It is a visual celebration of God's blessings for you as you join hands and lives to pursue together the riches of God's love.

Place
Wedding
Invitation
Here

Our Wedding Day

_____

and

_____

Were United in Marriage

_____
(Date)

_____
(Location)

_____
(Church Official)

Witnesses:

_____

_____

_____

Prayers From My Family and Friends

_____
_____
_____
_____
_____
_____
_____
_____
_____
_____
_____
_____
_____
_____
_____
_____
_____
_____
_____
_____
_____
_____
_____
_____
_____

Special Wedding Day Memories

As I Dressed

_____

_____

_____

The Walk Down the Aisle

_____

_____

The Ceremony

_____

_____

The Kiss!

_____

_____

The Reception

_____

_____

The Honeymoon

_____

_____

_____

Photo

The Fail-Safe Plan

The wedding ceremony is an expression of all the beauty and hope life has to offer. It is the beginning of a new life together— by choice—and it is deliberately and meticulously planned. But beyond the beautiful arrangements, silken fabrics, and sentimental gestures lies something more permanent than simply a day that passes away into memory. It is the bond of two believers with the Creator of their souls, and it is an invitation for His Spirit to guard and keep that which has been entrusted to Him on this special day.

Just as the actual ceremony takes time and effort to plan and prepare, so does the lifelong relationship that follows. Only through prayer and mutual submission to the Maker of marriage can marriage last. It is the one vital thread that keeps relationships strong, where all others would unravel. He is the strength in our weakness and the hope to which we cling. Pages have been provided for you to record your love and prayers for each other on this special occasion. May they serve as a reminder of the intensity of your love at this moment, and may the illustrations reflect the innocence of unmitigated devotion to each other and to God. As future triumphs and trials arise, may they also serve as a hallmark of hope and a reminder to remain committed to the love that you now feel so strongly.

Dear Heavenly Father,

We may plan, but You alone direct our steps. It is our hearts' desire that we honor You with our lives—not just on our wedding day, but every day that follows. Protect us from evil that would destroy the union You have created on this day. Empower us to work with Your Holy Spirit to establish Your kingdom on this earth through the love that You have afforded to both of us. Help us, in all things, to acknowledge You, that You may make our paths straight. We welcome You as an integral part of our relationship, and we look to You for the hope of our future.

In Jesus' name,

Amen

He who finds
a wife finds a
good thing,
and obtains favor
from the LORD.

Proverbs 18:22

Therefore a man shall leave his father and mother and be joined to his wife, and they shall become one flesh.

Genesis 2:24

*This is
My commandment,
that you love
one another as
I have loved
you.*

John 15:12

As the bridegroom
rejoices over
the bride,
so shall
your God
rejoice over you.

Isaiah 62:5

Wives, submit to your own husbands, as is fitting in the Lord. Husbands, love your wives and do not be bitter toward them.

Colossians 3:18-19

Who can find a
virtuous wife?
For her worth is far
above rubies.
The heart of her husband
safely trusts her;
so he will have no lack
of gain.

Proverbs 31:10-11

*Two are better
than one,
because they have
a good reward for
their labor.*

Ecclesiastes 4:9

I am my beloved's, and my beloved is mine.

Song of Solomon 6:3

You shall love the
LORD *your God with
all your heart,
with all your soul,
with all your mind,
and with all your
strength.*

Mark 12:30

Behold,
you are fair,
my love! . . .
Behold,
you are handsome,
my beloved!

Song of Solomon 1:15–16

So then, they are no longer two but one flesh. Therefore what God has joined together, let not man separate.

Matthew 19:6

"The LORD *bless you
and keep you;
The* LORD *make
His face shine upon you,
and be gracious to you;
the* LORD *lift up
His countenance upon you,
and give you peace."*

Numbers 6:24-26

*Let each one of you
in particular so love
his own wife as himself,
and let the wife
see that she respects
her husband.*

Ephesians 5:33

Beloved, let us love one another, for love is of God; and everyone who loves is born of God and knows God.

1 John 4:7

*Let the husband
render to his wife
the affection due her,
and likewise also
the wife to her
husband.*

1 Corinthians 7:3

*As for me
and my house,
we will serve
the LORD.*

Joshua 24:15

Be of good comfort,
be of one mind,
live in peace;
and the God of love
and peace will
be with you.

2 Corinthians 13:11

*And now abide
faith, hope, love,
these three;
but the greatest of
these is love.*

1 Corinthians 13:13

A Love Letter
For My Husband

A Love Letter
For My Wife

_____

_____

_____

_____

_____

_____

_____

_____

_____

_____

_____

_____

_____

_____

_____

_____

_____

_____

_____

_____

_____

_____

Two Hearts Together

Photo of Bride and Groom

Forever!

Wherever you go, I will go;
and wherever you lodge, I will
lodge; your people shall be my
people, and your God, my God.

Ruth 1:16